2ND EDITION

PIANO · VOCAL · GUITAR

WEDDING SONGS
OF LOVE & FRIENDSHIP

ISBN 978-1-4950-7244-4

T0087288

HAL•LEONARD

7777 W. BLUEMOUND RD. P.O. BOX 13819 MILWAUKEE, WI 53213

Visit Hal Leonard Online at
www.halleonard.com

CONTENTS

ALL I WANT IS YOU

Words by BONO and THE EDGE
Music by U2

Because You Loved Me
from UP CLOSE AND PERSONAL

Words and Music by
DIANE WARREN

Slowly

For all ___ those times you stood ___ by me, for all ___ the
wings and made ___ me fly. You touched ___ my

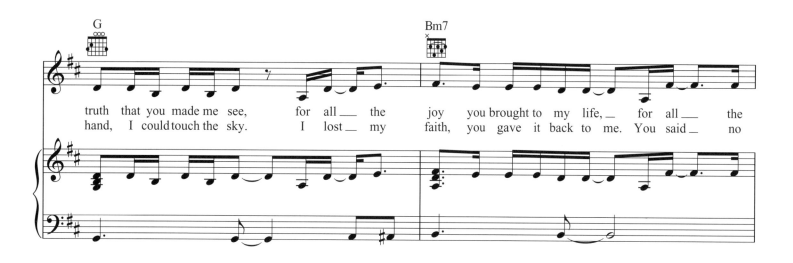

truth that you made me see, for all ___ the joy you brought to my life, ___ for all ___ the
hand, I could touch the sky. I lost ___ my faith, you gave it back to me. You said ___ no

wrong that you ___ made right, for ev - 'ry ___ dream you made ___ come true, for all ___ the
star was out ___ of reach. You stood ___ by ___ me and I ___ stood tall. I had ___ your

* Recorded a half step lower.

ALL OF ME

Words and Music by JOHN STEPHENS
and TOBY GAD

AND I LOVE HER

Words and Music by JOHN LENNON
and PAUL McCARTNEY

D.S. al Coda

have you near me.

CODA

Instrumental solo
Bright are the stars

that shine, dark is the sky.

I know this love of mine will nev-er die.

ANNIE'S SONG

Words and Music by
JOHN DENVER

AS TIME GOES BY
from CASABLANCA

Words and Music by
HERMAN HUPFELD

AT LAST
from ORCHESTRA WIVES

Lyric by MACK GORDON
Music by HARRY WARREN

I was nev-er spell-bound by a star-ry sky.

What is there to moon-glow, when love has passed you by?

Then there came a mid-night and the world was new. Now

BEAUTIFUL IN MY EYES

Words and Music by
JOSHUA KADISON

CAN'T HELP FALLING IN LOVE

from the Paramount Picture BLUE HAWAII

Words and Music by GEORGE DAVID WEISS,
HUGO PERETTI and LUIGI CREATORE

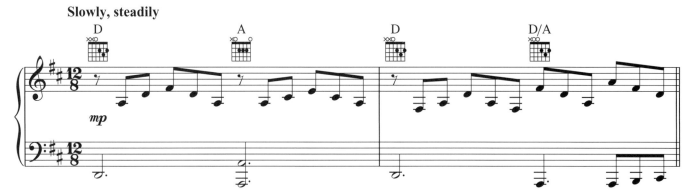

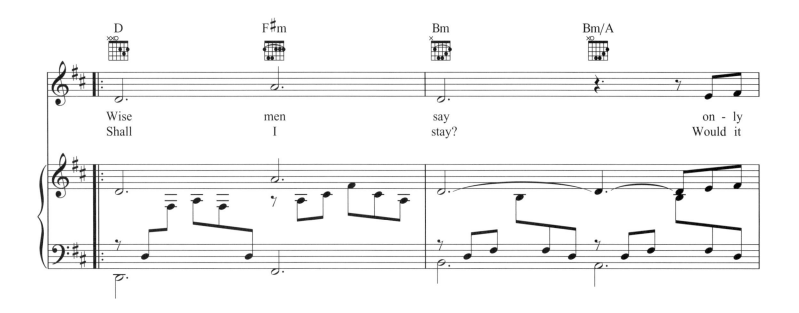

Wise men say only
Shall I stay? Would it

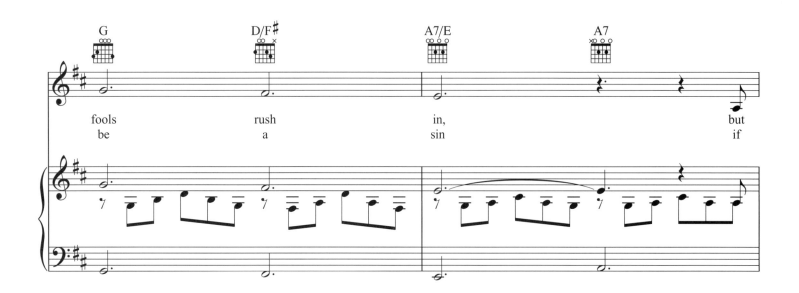

fools rush in, but
be a sin if

COME AWAY WITH ME

Words and Music by
NORAH JONES

Moderately slow

Come a-way with me in the night.

Come a-way with me and I will ____ write ____ you ____ a song ____

stop   lov - in'   you. _____

CHASING CARS

Words and Music by GARY LIGHTBODY,
TOM SIMPSON, PAUL WILSON,
JONATHAN QUINN and NATHAN CONNOLLY

DADDY DANCE WITH ME

Words and Music by KRYSTAL KEITH,
SONYA RUTLEDGE and MICA ROBERTS

* *Recorded a half step lower.*

COME RAIN OR COME SHINE

from ST. LOUIS WOMAN

Words by JOHNNY MERCER
Music by HAROLD ARLEN

Lyrics:
hap - py to - geth - er and won't it be fine. _____

Days may be cloud - y or sun - ny. We're in or we're out of the

mon - ey, but I'm with you al - ways, I'm with you rain ___ or

shine. _____

shine. _____

FIRST DAY OF MY LIFE

Words and Music by
CONOR OBERST

This is the first ___ day of ___ my life. ___
Re-mem-ber the time ___ you drove ___ all night ___

I swear I ___ was born right in ___ the door - way.
just ___ to meet ___ me in ___ the morn - ing?

I ONLY HAVE EYES FOR YOU

from DAMES

Words by AL DUBIN
Music by HARRY WARREN

Moderately

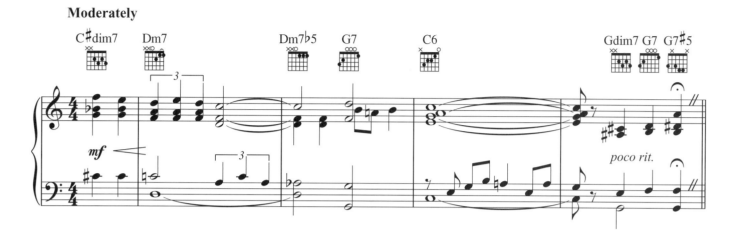

My love must be a kind of blind love, _____

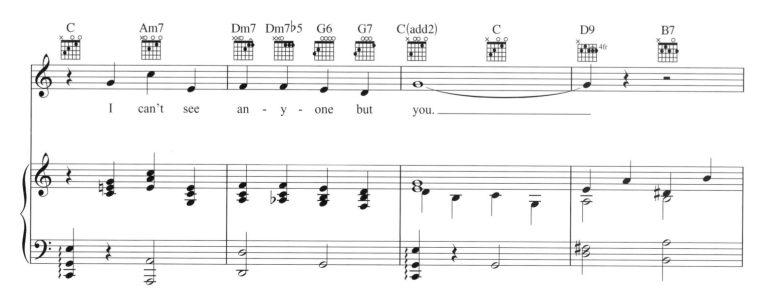

I can't see an-y-one but you. _____

And dear, I won-der if you find love

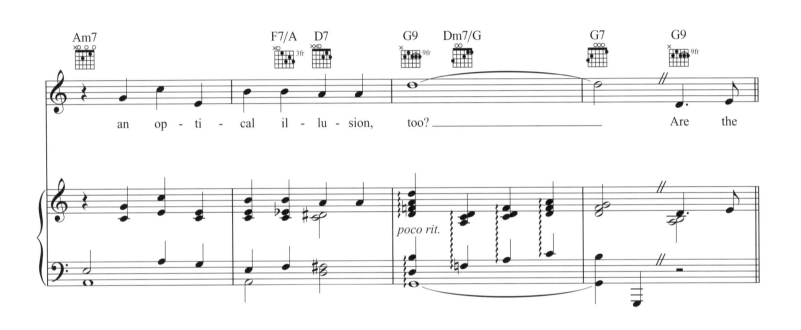

an op-ti-cal il-lu-sion, too? _____ Are the

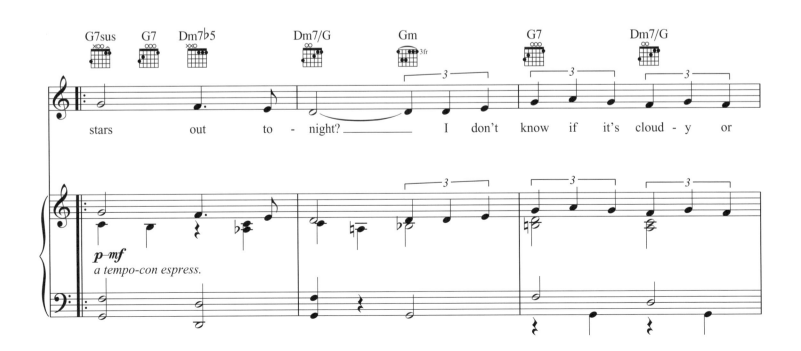

stars out to-night? _____ I don't know if it's cloud-y or

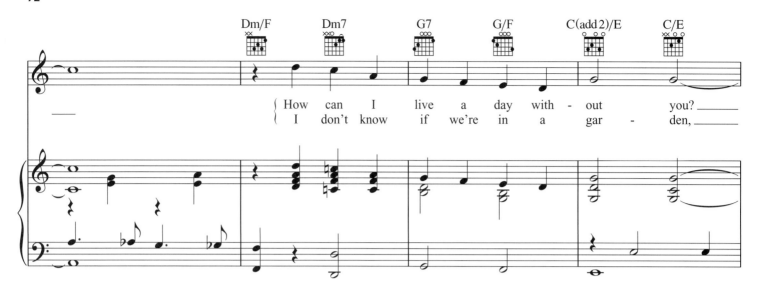

How can I live a day with - out you? _____
I don't know if we're in a gar - den, _____

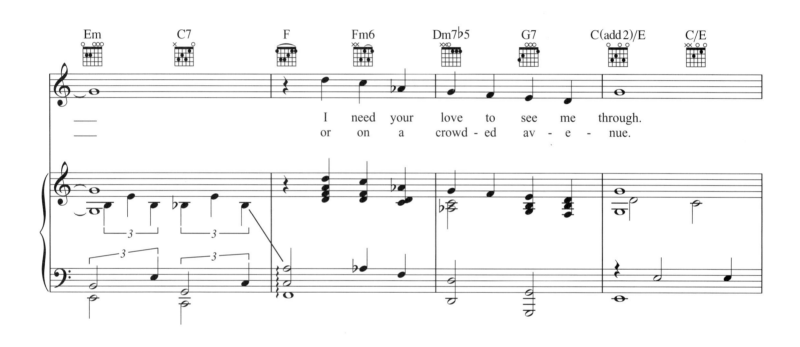

_____ I need your love to see me through.
_____ or on a crowd - ed av - e - nue.

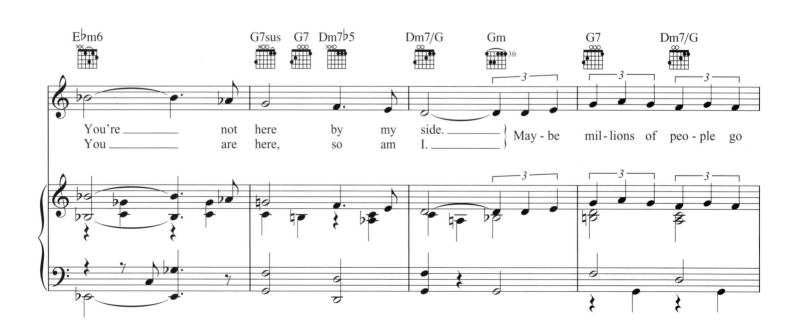

You're _____ not here by my side. _____
You _____ are here, so am I. _____ May - be mil - lions of peo - ple go

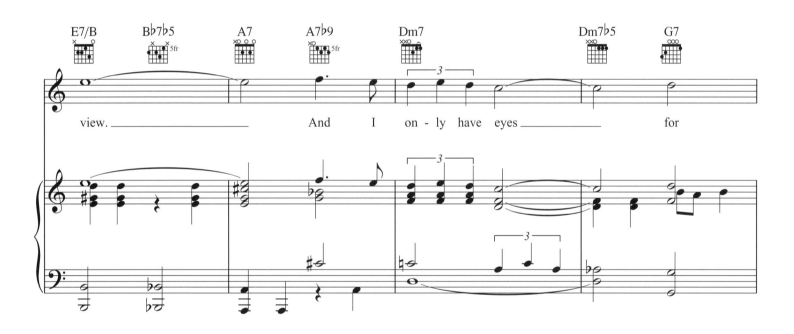

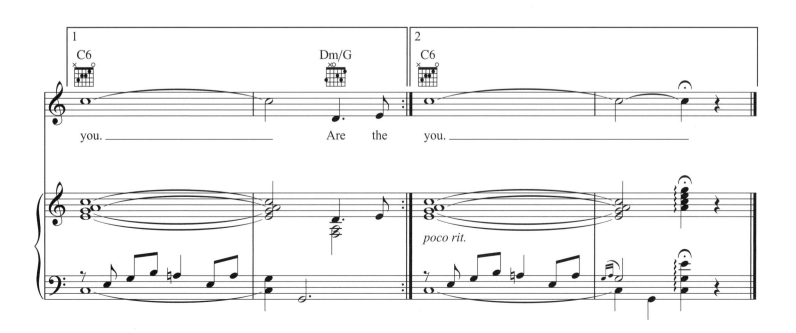

FOR YOU, FOR ME, FOR EVERMORE

Music and Lyrics by GEORGE GERSHWIN
and IRA GERSHWIN

Par - a - dise can-not re -

fuse us, nev - er such a hap - py pair!

Ev - 'ry-bod - y must ex - cuse us if we walk on

HOW LONG WILL I LOVE YOU

Words and Music by
MIKE SCOTT

Moderately slow

How long will I love you? As long as stars are a-bove you,

and long-er if I can.

How long will I need you? As long as the sea-sons need to

I GET TO LOVE YOU

Words and Music by MAGGIE ECKFORD
and MATT BRONLEEWE

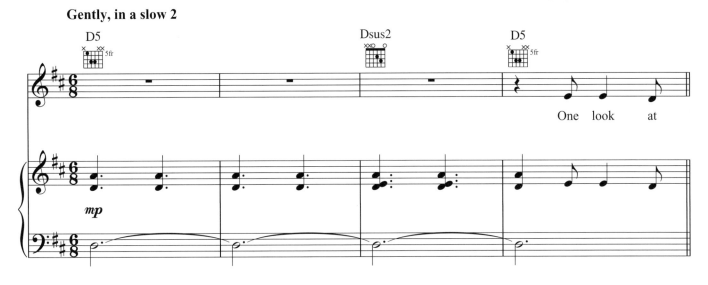

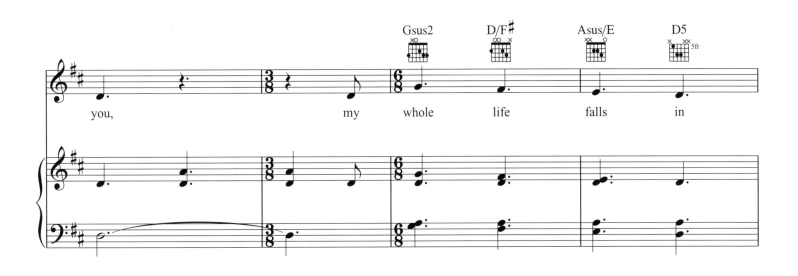

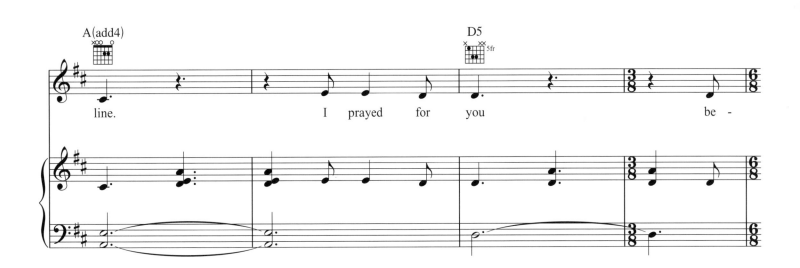

I WON'T GIVE UP

Words and Music by JASON MRAZ
and MICHAEL NATTER

*Guitarists: Tune 6th string down to D.

IT HAD TO BE YOU

Words by GUS KAHN
Music by ISHAM JONES

Moderate Swing

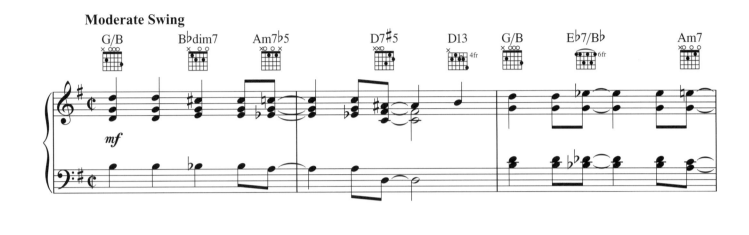

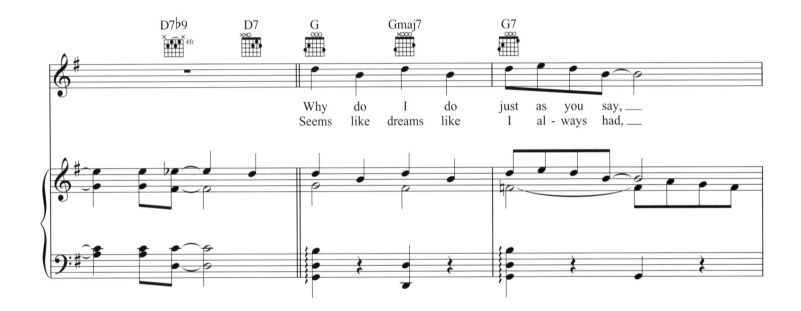

Why do I do just as you say, ___
Seems like dreams like I al-ways had, ___

why must I just give you your way? ___
could be, should be mak-ing me glad. ___

Why do I sigh, ___
Why am I blue? ___

why don't I try ___ to for - get? It must have
It's up to you ___ to ex - plain. I'm think - ing

been that some - thing lov - ers call fate ___ kept on say - ing
may - be, ba - by, I'll go a - way, ___ some - day, some way,

I had to wait. _ I saw them all, ___ just could - n't fall ___ 'til we
you'll come and say: _ "It's you I need, _ and you'll be plead - ing in

met. _____

vain. _____ } It had to be you, _____

_____ it had to be you, _____ I wan-dered a-round_____

_____ and fi-nal-ly found_____ the some-bod-y who_____

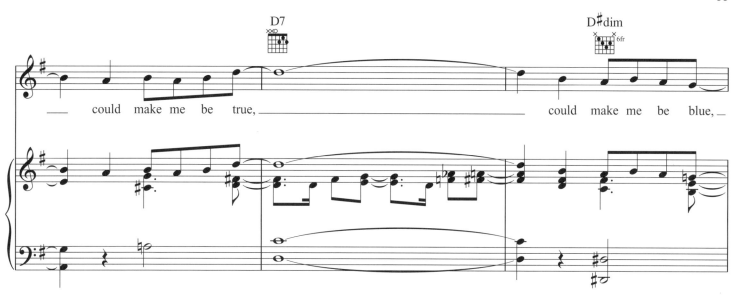

could make me be true, _____ could make me be blue, _____

_____ and e-ven be glad, _____ just to be sad, _

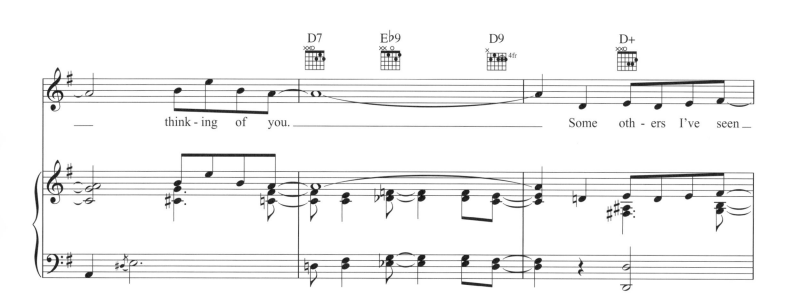

think-ing of you. _____ Some oth-ers I've seen _

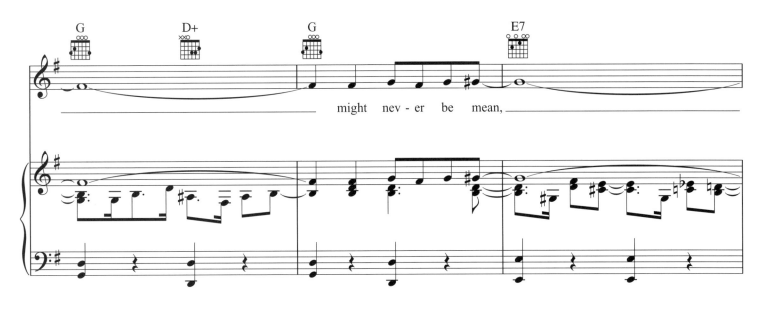

might nev-er be mean,

might nev-er be cross ___ or try to be boss, ___ but they would-n't do. ___

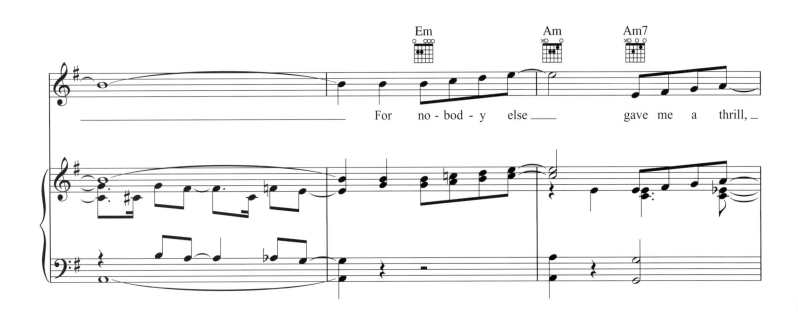

For no-bod-y else ___ gave me a thrill, ___

with all your faults __ I love you still, __ it had to be you, __

__ won - der - ful you, __ had to be you. __

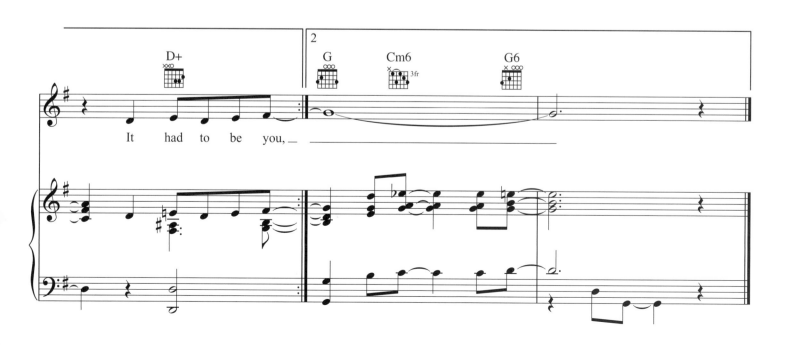

It had to be you, __ _____

LIKE I'M GONNA LOSE YOU

Words and Music by CAITLYN ELIZABETH SMITH,
JUSTIN WEAVER and MEGHAN TRAINOR

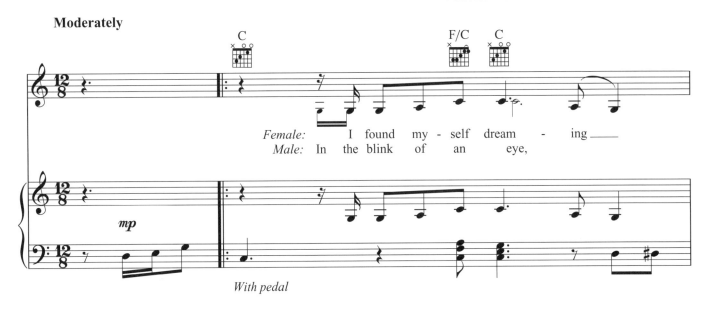

and you pulled me close. _____
an - y chance that I get. _____

Split sec - ond and you dis - ap - peared, and then
I'll make the most of the min - utes and

I was all a - lone. _____
love with no re - gret. _____

I woke up in tears with you by my side.
Let's take our time to say what we want,

Breath of re - lief, and I re - al - ized, _____
use what we've got be - fore it's all gone; _____

no, ___ we're not
'cause, no, ___ we're not

NEVER MY LOVE

Words and Music by DON ADDRISI
and DICK ADDRISI

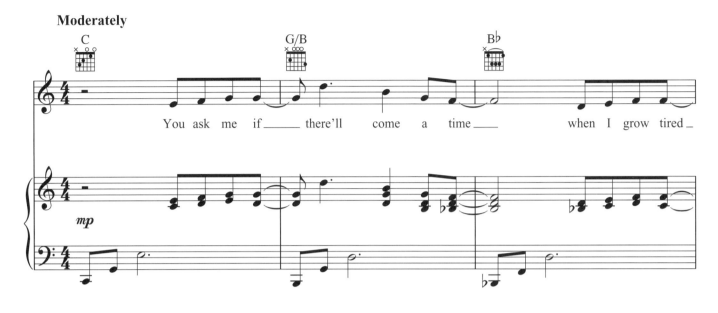

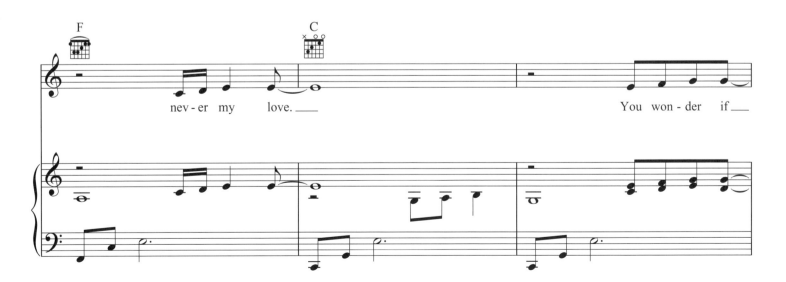

LONGER

Words and Music by
DAN FOGELBERG

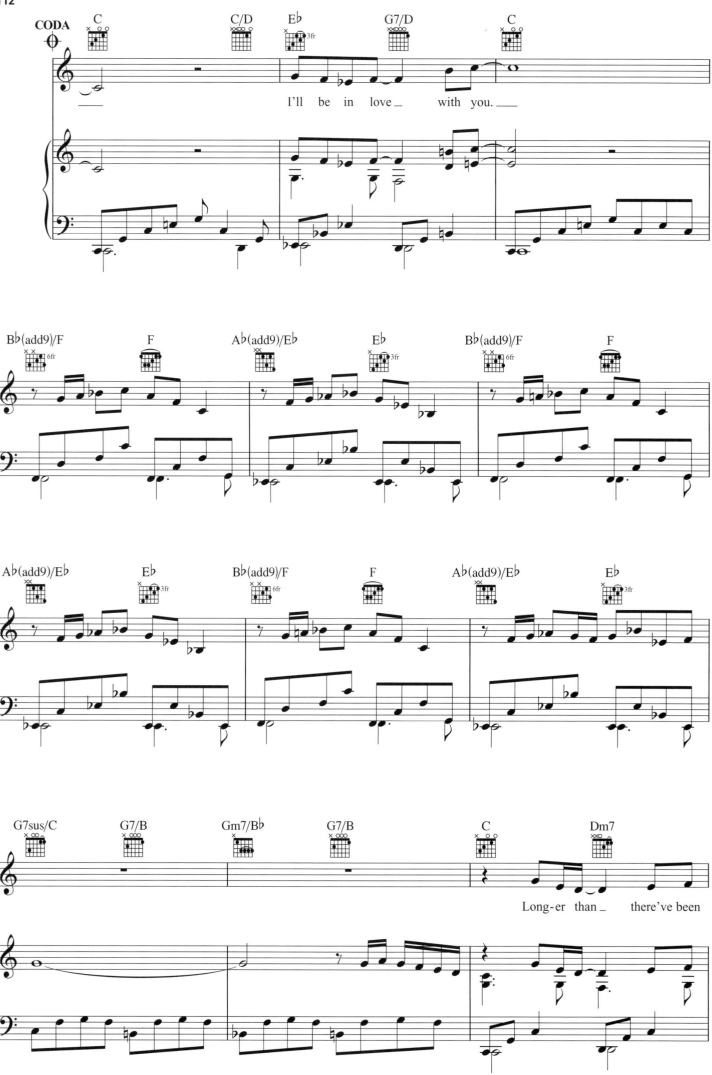

CODA

I'll be in love _ with you. _

Long-er than _ there've been

THE MAN YOU LOVE

Words and Music by STEVE MAC,
BLAIR DALEY and TROY VERGES

Slow Ballad

With pedal

Si me ves hal la-rás en mis o - jos el ___ a-mor. ___ E-res
tú la mi tad que a mi vi-da com - ple-to. ___ Lo que soy te da-ré sin
mie-do a al-gun ___ er - ror. ___ Creo en ti ___ y de-ja-ré en tus

love you for all my __ life. _____ I don't wan-na change the world. __

As long as you're __ my girl, __ it's more than e - nough _____

just to be the man __ you love.

decresc. (1st time only)

mp

Quie-ro

LOVESONG

Words and Music by ROBERT SMITH,
LAURENCE TOLHURST, SIMON GALLUP,
PAUL S. THOMPSON, BORIS WILLIAMS
and ROGER O'DONNELL

Slow groove

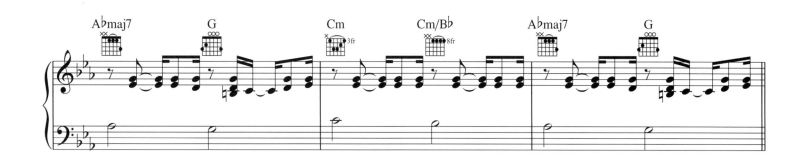

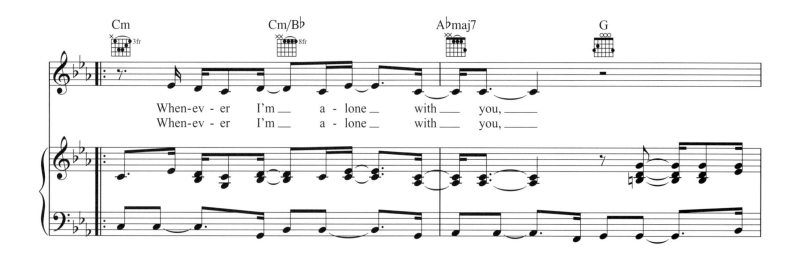

When-ev-er I'm __ a - lone __ with __ you, __
When-ev-er I'm __ a - lone __ with __ you, __

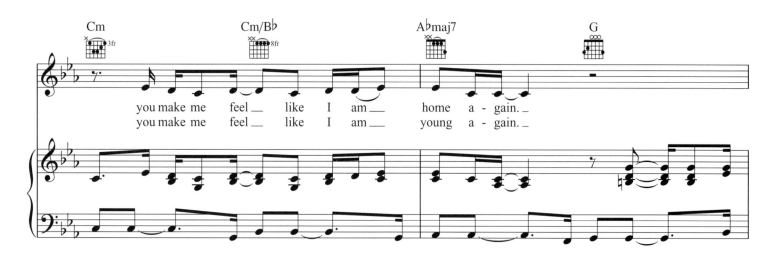

you make me feel __ like I am __ home a - gain. __
you make me feel __ like I am __ young a - gain. __

When-ev - er I'm __ a - lone __ with __ you, _____
When-ev - er I'm __ a - lone __ with __ you, _____

you make me feel __ like I am __ whole a - gain. __
you make me feel __ like I am __

you, I'll al - ways __ love you. __ I'll al - ways __

__ love you. __ 'Cause I love __ you. __

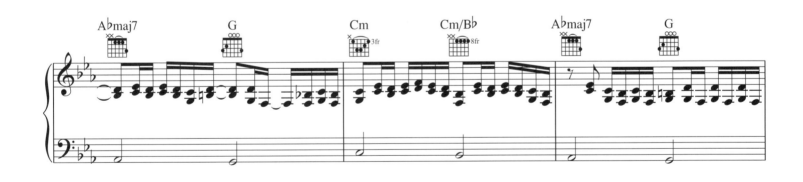

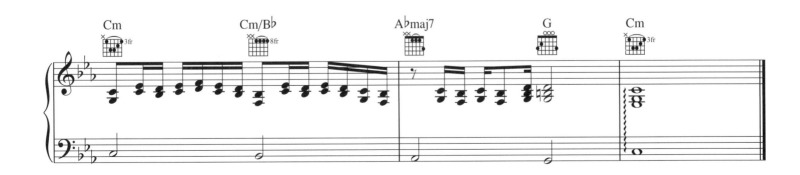

ONCE IN A LIFETIME

Words and Music by JOHN SHANKS
and KEITH URBAN

ONE CALL AWAY

Words and Music by CHARLIE PUTH,
BREYAN ISAAC, MATT PRIME,
JUSTIN FRANKS, BLAKE ANTHONY CARTER
and MAUREEN McDONALD

* *Recorded a half step higher.*

now, we can stay ___ here for ___ a while ___ 'cause, you know, ___ I just wan - na see ___ you smile. _____ No mat - ter where ___ you go, ___ you know you're not ___ a - lone. I'm on - ly ___ one call a - way, _____ I'll be there to

OVER AND OVER AGAIN

Words and Music by HELEN CULVER,
HARMONY SAMUELS, NATHAN SYKES
and MAJOR JOHNSON

Driving Piano Ballad

THE PROMISE
(I'll Never Say Goodbye)
Theme from the Universal Picture THE PROMISE

Words by ALAN and MARILYN BERGMAN
Music by DAVID SHIRE

Cue notes optional 2nd time

STAND BY YOU

Words and Music by RACHEL PLATTEN,
JOY WILLIAMS, JACK ANTONOFF,
JON LEVINE and MATTHEW B. MORRIS

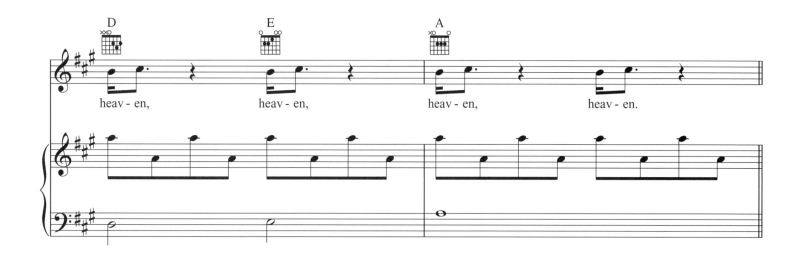

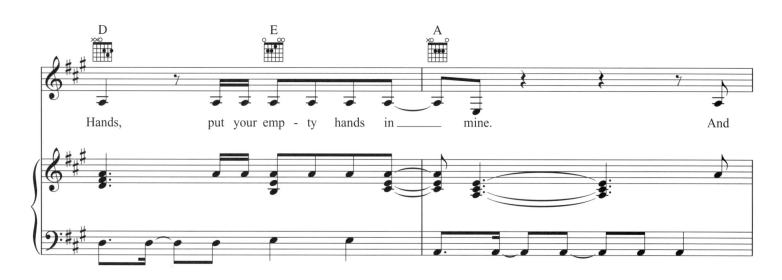

I,_____ I'm gon-na stand by you. E - ven if we're break - ing

down, __ we can find a way to break through. __ E - ven if we can't find

heav - en, I'll walk through hell with you. Love,_____ you're not a - lone, __

__ 'cause I'm gon - na stand by you._____ E - ven if we can't find

SWEETEST DEVOTION

Words and Music by ADELE ADKINS
and PAUL EPWORTH

Slowly, in 2

THINKING OUT LOUD

Words and Music by ED SHEERAN
and AMY WADGE

TURNING PAGE

from the Summit Entertainment film THE TWILIGHT SAGA: BREAKING DAWN – PART 1

Words and Music by
RYAN CURTIS O'NEAL

Moderately slow

Pedal ad lib. throughout

I've wait-ed a hun-dred years, but I'd wait ___ a mil-lion more for you.

Your love is my turn - ing page, where on - ly the sweet-est words _ re-

Abmaj9   Abmaj13   Abmaj9   Abmaj13

main.

Eb   Gm/D   Cm7   Gm/Bb

Ev-'ry kiss is a cur - sive line, _ ev-'ry touch is a re - de - fined _____

Abmaj9   Abmaj13   Abmaj9   Abmaj13

_____ phrase.

THIS I PROMISE YOU

Words and Music by RONAN KEATING,
PAUL BARRY and MARK TAYLOR

A THOUSAND YEARS

from the Summit Entertainment film THE TWILIGHT SAGA: BREAKING DAWN – Part 1

Words and Music by DAVID HODGES
and CHRISTINA PERRI

I'll love you for ___ a thou - sand

more. ___

TRULY, MADLY, DEEPLY

Words and Music by DANIEL JONES
and DARREN HAYES

UNFORGETTABLE

Words and Music by
IRVING GORDON

YOU ARE THE SUNSHINE
OF MY LIFE

Words and Music by
STEVIE WONDER

WHO I AM WITH YOU

Words and Music by JASON SELLERS,
PAUL JENKINS and MARV GREEN

YOU AND ME

Words and Music by JASON WADE
and JUDE COLE

YOU ARE SO BEAUTIFUL

Words and Music by BILLY PRESTON
and BRUCE FISHER

Moderately slow, expressively

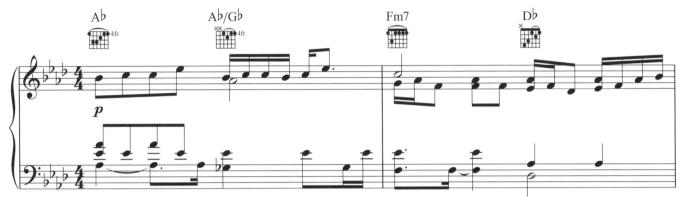

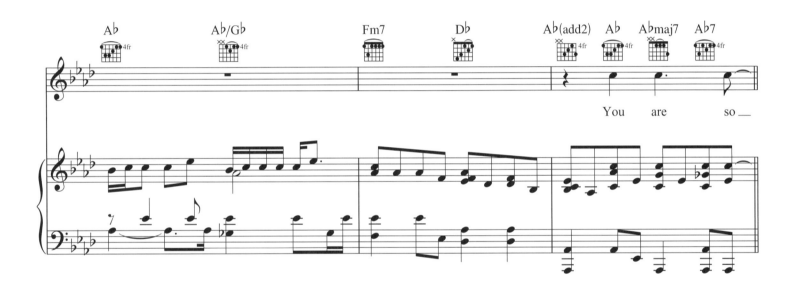

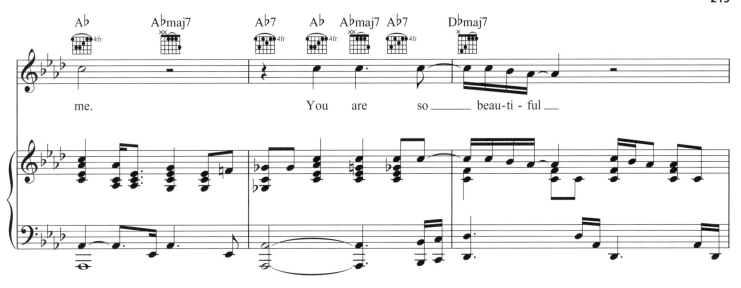

me. You are so _____ beau-ti - ful _____

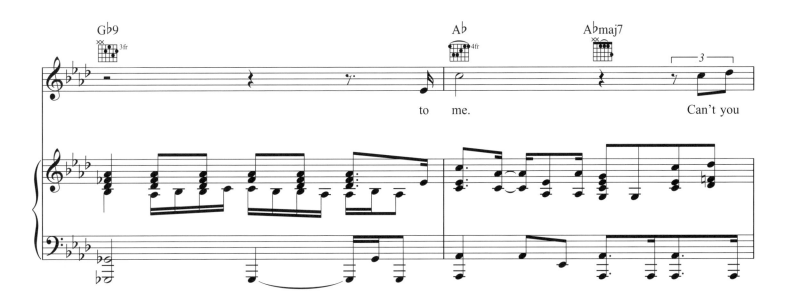

to me. Can't you

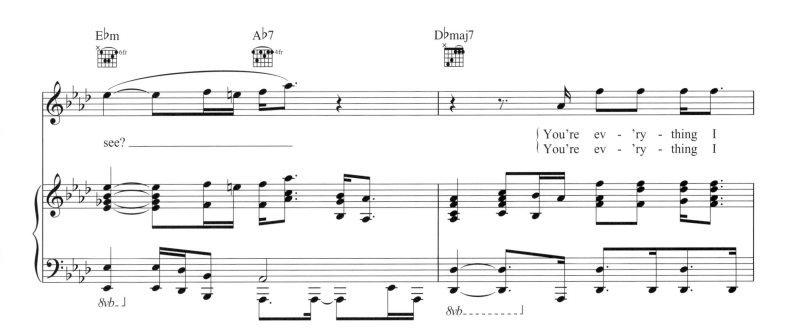

see? _____

You're ev - 'ry - thing I
You're ev - 'ry - thing I

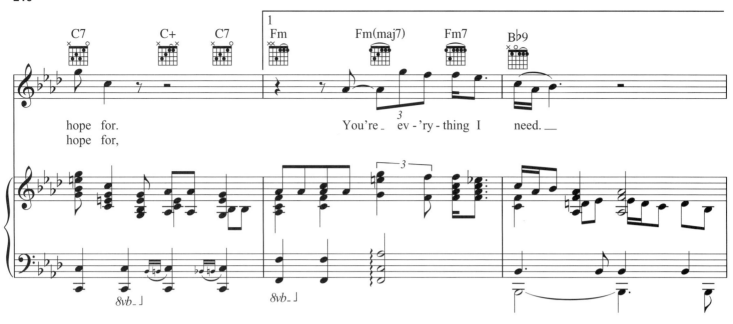

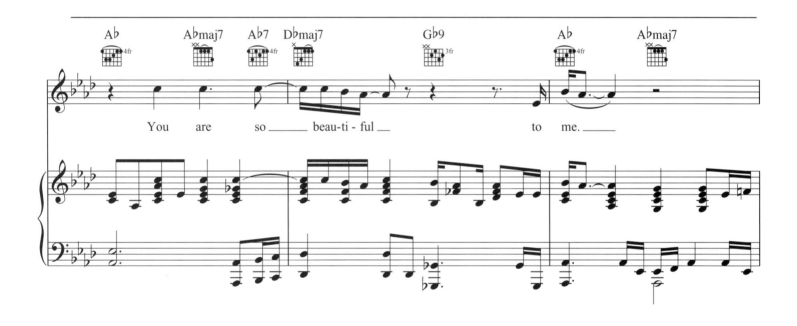

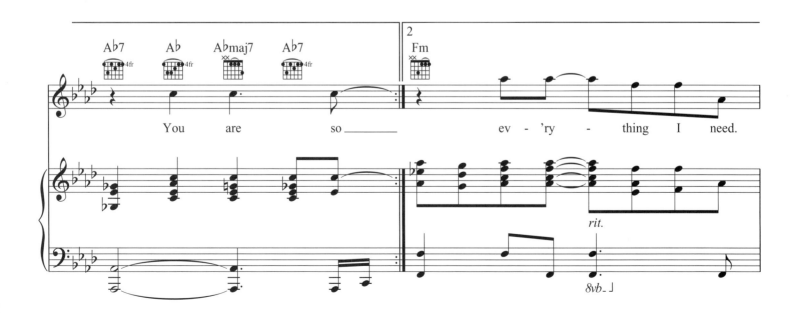

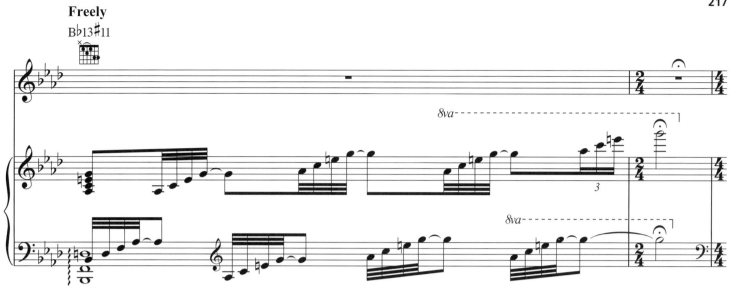

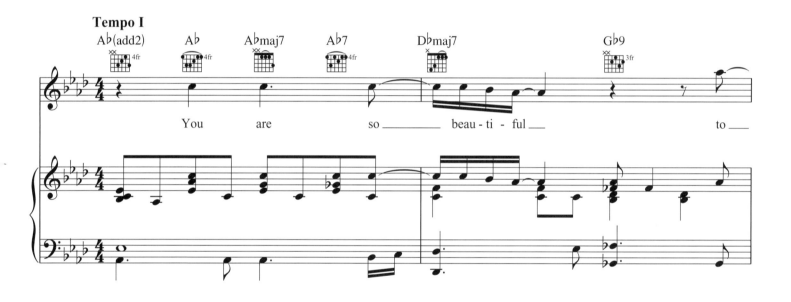

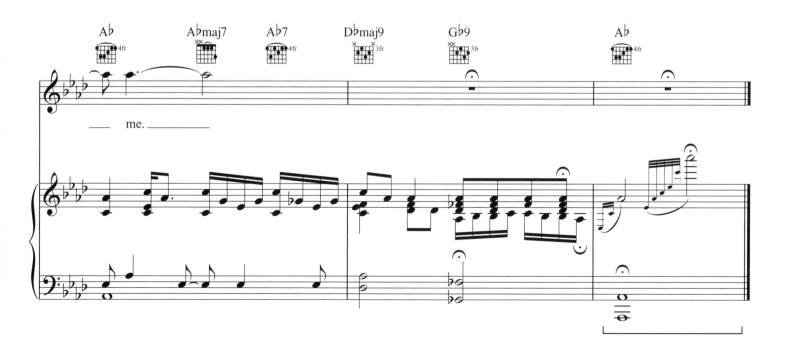

YOU'RE MY BEST FRIEND

Words and Music by
JOHN DEACON

With a beat

The Most Romantic Music In The World

Arranged for piano, voice, and guitar

The Best Love Songs Ever – 2nd Edition

This revised edition includes 65 romantic favorites: Always • Beautiful in My Eyes • Can You Feel the Love Tonight • Endless Love • Have I Told You Lately • Misty • Something • Through the Years • Truly • When I Fall in Love • and more.

00359198 .... $19.99

The Big Book of Love Songs – 2nd Edition

80 romantic hits in many musical styles: Always on My Mind • Cherish • Fields of Gold • I Honestly Love You • I'll Be There • Isn't It Romantic? • Lady • My Heart Will Go On • Save the Best for Last • Truly • Wonderful Tonight • and more.

00310784 .... $19.95

The Bride's Wedding Music Collection

A great collection of popular, classical and sacred songs for wedding musicians or engaged couples who are planning their service. Over 40 categorized songs, plus a website to hear audio clips! Songs include: Bless the Broken Road • Canon in D • Everything • Grow Old with Me • In My Life • Jesu, Joy of Man's Desiring • The Lord's Prayer • Marry Me • Ode to Joy • When You Say Nothing at All • and more.

00312298 .... $17.99

The Bride's Guide to Wedding Music – 2nd Edition

This great guide is a complete resource for planning wedding music. It includes a thorough article on choosing music for a wedding ceremony, and 65 songs in many different styles to satisfy lots of different tastes. The songs are grouped by categories, including preludes, processionals, recessionals, traditional sacred songs, popular songs, country songs, contemporary Christian songs, Broadway numbers, and new age piano music.

00310615 .... $19.95

Disney's Fairy Tale Weddings

Features 14 romantic ballads from Disney favorites: Beauty and the Beast • Bella Notte (This Is the Night) • Can You Feel the Love Tonight • Part of Your World • Some Day My Prince Will Come • When You Wish upon a Star • A Whole New World • and more!

00313588 .... $14.99

Love Songs
Budget Books Series

74 favorite love songs, including: And I Love Her • Cherish • Crazy • Endless Love • Fields of Gold • I Just Called to Say I Love You • I'll Be There • (You Make Me Feel Like) A Natural Woman • Wonderful Tonight • You Are So Beautiful • and more.

00310834 .... $12.99

Modern Love Songs

27 recent hits, including: Just a Kiss (Lady Antebellum) • Just the Way You Are (Bruno Mars) • Love Somebody (Maroon 5) • Marry Me (Train) • No One (Alicia Keys) • Ours (Taylor Swift) • Stay (Rihanna) • A Thousand Years (Christina Perri) • Unconditionally (Katy Perry) • Wanted (Hunter Hayes) • and more.

00127068 .... $17.99

Modern Wedding Songs

27 contemporary wedding requests, including: All of Me • Are You Gonna Kiss Me or Not • God Gave Me You • I Choose You • Lost in This Moment • Love Someone • Marry Me • Marry You • A Thousand Years • Who You Love • You and Me • You Are the Best Thing • and more.

00138577... $17.99

Romance – Boleros Favoritos

Features 48 Spanish and Latin American favorites: Aquellos Ojos Verdes • Bésame Mucho • El Reloj • Frenes • Inolvidable • La Vida Es Un Sueño • Perfidia • Siempre En Mi Corazón • Solamente Una Vez • more.

00310383 .... $17.99

Romantic Sheet Music Collection

Over 30 songs perfect for expressing that loving feeling, including: At Last • Can't Help Falling in Love • Crazy Love • First Day of My Life • I Just Called to Say I Love You • In Your Eyes • Let's Stay Together • Maybe I'm Amazed • Sea of Love • Thinking Out Loud • Unchained Melody • Your Song • and more.

00148757... $16.99

Songs from the Heart

40 songs about love and friendship, including: Annie's Song • Don't Know Much • Endless Love • Faithfully • Hello • I Will Always Love You • I'll Have to Say I Love You in a Song • Just the Way You Are • Longer • More Than Words • Right Here Waiting • That's What Friends Are For • The Wind Beneath My Wings • and more.

00121512... $17.99

Today's Hits for Weddings

Contains 25 of today's best pop and country hits that are perfect for weddings! Includes: Bless the Broken Road • Everything • Halo • I Do • Just the Way You Are • Love Story • Lucky • Marry Me • Mine • River of Love • Today Was a Fairytale • You Raise Me Up • and more.

00312316 .... $16.99

Valentine

Let your love light shine with this collection of 50 romantic favorites! Includes: Can't Help Falling and Love • Endless Love • If • Just the Way You Are • L-O-V-E • Mona Lisa • My Funny Valentine • Something • Three Coins in the Fountain • We've Only Just Begun • You Are So Beautiful • You'll Accomp'ny Me • and more!

00310977 .... $16.95

Selections from
VH1's 100 Greatest Love Songs

Nearly 100 love songs chosen for their emotion. Includes: Always on My Mind • Baby, I Love Your Way • Careless Whisper • Endless Love • How Deep Is Your Love • I Got You Babe • If You Leave Me Now • Love Me Tender • My Heart Will Go On • Unchained Melody • You're Still the One • and dozens more!

00306506 .... $27.95

HAL•LEONARD®

www.halleonard.com